H O W
T O

gain confidence

A How to Book by

L.A. Dawn

TABLE OF CONTENTS

- *1 Life* — III
- *2 Insecurities* — IV
- *3. Doubt* — V
- *4 Opinions* — VI
- *5 Reassurance* — VII
- *6 Mistakes* — VIII
- *7 Self Reflection* — IX
- *8 Self Improvement* — X
- *9 Self Love* — XI
- *10 Focus* — XII
- *11 Trust Yourself* — XIII

Conclusion — XIV

HOW TO...

Introduction

WHAT DOES HE/SHE HAVE THAT I DON'T?
DO YOU NEED HELP BUILDING CONFIDENCE?
LEARN HOW TO MASTER THE ESSENTIAL KEYS TO
BEING CONFIDENT.
I REALIZED A LOT OF PEOPLE HAVE NO CLUE
WHAT THAT "JE NE SAIS QUOI" IS. WELL I DO.
"HOW TO GROW CONFIDENCE" PROVIDES YOU WITH
THE FOUNDATION YOU WILL NEED. EACH CHAPTER
GIVES YOU USEFUL INFO ALONG WITH A WORD, A
GOAL, AND AN AFFIRMATION FOR THAT DAY.
WELCOME TO THE FIRST DAY OF YOUR NEW
CONFIDENT LIFE.

CHAPTER
ONE

LIFE

NOT TO SOUND CLICHE, BUT "LIFE" IS REALLY WHAT
YOU MAKE IT. SURE, YOU CAN'T JUST WAKE UP
EVERYDAY AND DEMAND IT TO BE A PERFECT DAY
AND THATS EXACTLY WHAT ENDS UP HAPPENING.
SOME DAYS WILL BE PERFECT WHILE OTHERS WILL
DEFINITELY NOT BE! THE MOST IMPORTANT THING
TO REMEMBER IS THAT YOU HAVE THE POWER TO
LET THE BAD THINGS CONSUME YOU OR NOT. TRUTH
IS EVERYONE GOES THROUGH TRIALS AND
TRIBULATIONS AT SOME POINT IN LIFE. SOME MORE
THAN OTHERS. NO MATTER WHAT RACE, GENDER,
RELIGION, ETC. IT IS INEVITABLE. LIFE IS MEANT TO
BE LIVED. SO LET'S MAKE THAT PROMISE TO
OURSELVES.

WORD OF THE DAY : LIVE
GOAL OF THE DAY : WRITE DOWN A FEW HOBBIES THAT
YOU ENJOY DOING.
AFFIRMATION OF THE DAY: 'LIFE IS GOOD'

Reflection:

III

CHAPTER
TWO

INSECURITIES

JUST LIKE AN OPINION, EVERYBODY HAS ONE OR TWO.OR 20!. THAT'S JUST THE TRUTH. THE WAY I'VE LEARNED TO DEAL WITH MINE IS TO CHANGE THE ONES I CAN AND ACCEPT THE ONES I CAN'T. HONESTLY WHAT OTHER OPTIONS DO WE HAVE. YOU KNOW THAT SAYING."YOU WANT WHAT YOU CAN'T HAVE". NOWADAYS EVERYBODY IS SO CAUGHT UP WITH EVERYONE ELSE'S "THINGS". I THINK SOCIAL MEDIA PLAYS A HUGE PART IN THAT. DON'T GET ME WRONG, SOCIAL MEDIA CAN BE VERY INSPIRING AND UPLIFTING IF YOU ALLOW IT. I PERSONALLY LOOK IN THE MIRROR AND GET DOWN ON MYSELF BECAUSE I WOULD LOVE TO LOSE A FEW INCHES OFF MY TUMMY. THEN I'LL TURN AROUND AND EAT TWINKIES LIKE THEY'RE GOING OUT OF STYLE. SO I'M THE ONLY ONE TO BLAME IN THIS CASE. THAT'S ONE OF THOSE THINGS I CAN ACCEPT OR CHANGE.

WORD OF THE DAY: CHANGE
GOAL OF THE DAY: MAKE A LIST OF THINGS YOU ARE INSECURE ABOUT AND DECIDE IF YOU CAN CHANGE THEM OR IF YOU SHOULD JUST ACCEPT THEM.
AFFIRMATION: THERE IS ONLY ONE OF ME AND I LOVE ME!

Reflection:

CHAPTER
THREE

DOUBT

DOUBT: A FEELING OF UNCERTAINTY OR LACK OF CONVICTION SHOW OF HANDS OF HOW MANY OF US EVER EXPERIENCED THIS BEFORE. ALL OF US, RIGHT. DOUBT IS AN OBSTACLE THAT WE ALL HAVE TO FACE AND OVERCOME ALMOST EVERYDAY. THERE IS NO WAY AROUND IT. YOUR FAVORITE MOVIE STAR, WRITER, VLOGGER EVERYONE DONT LET "DOUBT BE THE REASON TO NOT FOLLOW THROUGH WITH SOMETHING YOU WANT TO DO. IF SOME OF THE MOST SUCCESSFUL PEOPLE WE KNOW WOULD HAVE LET "DOUBT" STOP THEM, WE WOULD BE WITHOUT SOME OF THE GREATEST INVENTIONS AND DEVICES WE HAVE TODAY. TOO MUCH "DOUBT" IS A HUGE CONFIDENCE KILLER LETS SAY YOU SEE A SHIRT IN A DEPARTMENT STORE AND YOUR INITIAL THOUGHT IS :OH MAN THAT IS A NICE SHIRT, I LOVE IT."

THEN YOU BEGIN TO WONDER IF THIS PERSON WILL LIKE OR IF PEOPLE WILL KNOW YOU GOT IT OFF THE SALES RACK ASK YOURSELF WHY YOU DO CARE? IF YOU LOVE IT , GET IT. THAT FEELING YOU HAD WHEN YOU FIRST SAW IT WILL COME OUT OF YOU WHEN YOU WEAR IT.

WORD OF THE DAY: TRUST
GOAL OF THE DAY: BE AWARE OF YOUR THOUGHTS THAT ARE FOLLOWED BY DOUBTS.
AFFIRMATION: I TRUST MYSELF TO MAKE THE BEST DECISIONS FOR ME!

Reflection:

v

OPINIONS

LET'S TALK ABOUT OTHER PEOPLE'S OPINIONS. THEY WILL ALWAYS HAVE A FEW. IM SURE YOU'VE HAD AN OPINION OR TWO ESPECIALLY WHEN IT COMES TO A FRIEND WHEN THEY ASK SHOULD THEY GIVE THEIR EX ANOTHER CHANCE IF YOU'RE LIKE ME YOU'LL GIVE THEM ADVICE BUT NEVER TELL THEM WHAT TO DO IN THEIR PERSONAL LIFE. LET'S FACE IT, THEY WILL DO WHAT THEY WANT IN THE END ANYWAY. SO THATS THE ONLY POINT I HAVE TO MAKE ABOUT OPINIONS. DO WHAT YOU WANT!! AS LONG AS IT'S NOT PHYSICALLY HARMFUL TO YOU OR ANYONE ELSE THATS ALL I HAVE TO SAY ABOUT THAT AND THATS EXACTLY HOW LONG YOU SHOULD LET ANOTHER PERSONS OPINION BOTHER YOU.

WORD OF THE DAY: BELIEF
GOAL OF THE DAY: REMIND YOURSELF THAT OPINIONS ARE LIKE A***'S EVERYBODY HAS ONE!
AFFIRMATION: IT DOESNT MATTER WHAT YOU THINK OF MEIT MATTERS WHAT I THINK OF ME

Reflection:

CHAPTER
FIVE

REASSURANCE

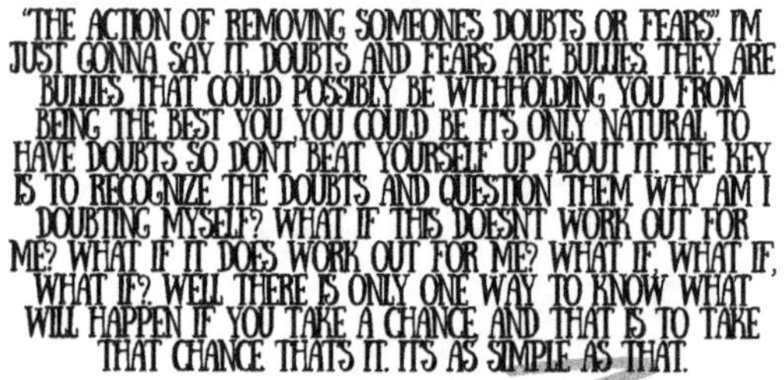

"THE ACTION OF REMOVING SOMEONE'S DOUBTS OR FEARS". I'M JUST GONNA SAY IT, DOUBTS AND FEARS ARE BULLIES. THEY ARE BULLIES THAT COULD POSSIBLY BE WITHHOLDING YOU FROM BEING THE BEST YOU, YOU COULD BE. IT'S ONLY NATURAL TO HAVE DOUBTS SO DON'T BEAT YOURSELF UP ABOUT IT. THE KEY IS TO RECOGNIZE THE DOUBTS AND QUESTION THEM. WHY AM I DOUBTING MYSELF? WHAT IF THIS DOESN'T WORK OUT FOR ME? WHAT IF IT DOES WORK OUT FOR ME? WHAT IF, WHAT IF, WHAT IF? WELL THERE IS ONLY ONE WAY TO KNOW WHAT WILL HAPPEN IF YOU TAKE A CHANCE AND THAT IS TO TAKE THAT CHANCE. THATS IT. ITS AS SIMPLE AS THAT.

WORD OF THE DAY: CHANCE
GOAL OF THE DAY: REFLECT ON A FEW THINGS THATS BEEN ON YOUR BUCKET-LIST AND MAKE THE EFFORT TO TAKE A CHANCE ON ONE
AFFIRMATION OF THE DAY: MY DOUBTS WILL NOT BEAT ME.

Reflection:

CHAPTER
SIX

MISTAKES

I HAVE MADE MILLIONS (MAYBE NOT THAT MANY) , BUT I'VE MADE A FEW. IT BUILDS CHARACTER NO MATTER HOW CHEESY THAT SOUNDS ITS TRUE. THE PERSON YOU ARE TODAY IS A REFLECTION OF THE DECISIONS AND CHOICES YOU MADE IN YOUR PAST. EVERYTHING THAT HAPPENS IN LIFE CAN BE USED AS A LESSON IF YOU LET IT. JUST TAKE SOME TIME TO EXAMINE WHAT HAPPENED, HOW IT MAKES YOU FEEL, WHAT YOU WOULD DO DIFFERENT OR NOT. KEEP IN MIND THAT ITS OK TO BE A LITTLE SELFISH WHEN IT COMES TO YOUR HEALTH AND WELL BEING LIKE PROBLEMS MISTAKES COME IN ALL DIFFERENT SHAPES AND SIZES ONE PERSONS HUGE MISTAKE COULD BE THE NEXT PERSONS SMALL MISTAKE ITS ALL ABOUT PERSPECTIVE WHICH GOES TO SHOW YOU ITS ALL ABOUT WHAT YOU MAKE OF IT. SO BE MINDFUL

WORD OF THE DAY: AWARE
GOAL OF THE DAY: THINK OF A MISTAKE YOU'VE MADE, BIG OR SMALL AND EXAMINE IT
AFFIRMATION OF THE DAY: I AM NOT MY MISTAKES!

Reflection:

CHAPTER SEVEN

SELF REFLECTION

SELF REFLECTION IS SO IMPORTANT. IF YOU DON'T KNOW WHO YOU ARE HOW THE HELL IS ANYBODY ELSE GOING TO GET TO KNOW YOU. KNOWING WHO YOU ARE IS A SECRET POWER (IN CASE YOU DIDN'T KNOW). IM PRETTY SURE WHEN YOU HEAR "KNOW YOURSELF" YOU MAY THINK IT'S A LITTLE "HIPPIE-ISH", BUT IT IS A HUGE PIECE TO THE PUZZLE OF BEING CONFIDENT. KNOWING WHO YOU ARE IS KNOWING WHAT YOU LIKE, DISLIKE, WHAT MAKES YOU HAPPY, WHAT MAKES YOU SAD, WHAT TURNS YOU ON, WHAT TURNS YOU OFF. WHEN YOU UNDERSTAND WHAT THOSE THINGS ARE YOU CAN EITHER ACCEPT THEM OR START TO MAKE THE CHANGES. KEEP AT THOSE CHANGES UNTIL YOU GET TO THE POINT OF WHERE YOU CAN LOVE IT OR YOU'RE OK WITH IT. EVERYBODY HAS SH*T THEY DON'T LIKE ABOUT THEMSELVES THE DIFFERENCE IS SOME JUST DON'T GIVE A DAMN HOW ANYBODY ELSE SEES THEM. THAT'S THE GOAL. THAT'S THE KEY.

WORD OF THE DAY: IMPERFECTIONS
GOAL OF THE DAY: WRITE DOWN THINGS YOU DON'T LIKE ABOUT YOURSELF AND FIGURE OUT IF THERE IS ANYTHING YOU CAN CHANGE OR IF YOU SHOULD WORK ON ACCEPTING AND BEING OK WITH IT.
AFFIRMATION OF THE DAY: I AM WHAT I THINK I AM.

Reflection:

CHAPTER
EIGHT

SELF IMPROVEMENT

THIS IS DEFINITELY A MARATHON AND NOT A SPRINT. YOU JUST HAVE TO BE CONSISTENT. SOME OF US ARE GOOD AT JUGGLING MULTIPLE THINGS AT ONCE AND OTHERS NOT SO MUCH.THAT'S TOTALLY FINE. NEVER COMPARE YOURSELF TO ANYONE ELSE. YOU ARE YOU. PERIOD. START OFF SLOWLY MAYBE CHOOSE ONE SMALL THING THAT YOU WANT TO CHANGE ABOUT YOURSELF. TRY TO CHOOSE SOMETHING THAT WON'T TAKE TOO LONG TO ACHIEVE. THAT WAY YOU WILL START TO BUILD CONFIDENCE BY ACCOMPLISHING THINGS YOU SET OUT TO ACCOMPLISH. IF YOU WANNA LOSE 15 POUNDS, START WITH A GOAL OF LOSING 5. SAY YOU WANT TO EAT BETTER, DON'T TRY AND ELIMINATE ALL BAD FOODS AT ONCE. THAT IS OVERWHELMING. NOW I KNOW THERE ARE FOLKS OUT THERE THAT CAN STOP COLD TURKEY AND THATS FREAKIN' AWESOME. JUST DO YOU. TRY NOT TO USE SOME DIET YOU SAW YOUR FAVORITE TV STAR DROP 1000 POUNDS IN 3 DAYS ON. DO YOUR RESEARCH ON DIFFERENT FOODS, WRITE DOWN WHAT FOODS YOU LIKE, CHECK OUT VIDEOS ABOUT DIFFERENT WORKOUTS AND FIGURE OUT WHAT YOUR "THING" IS.

WORD OF THE DAY: ME
GOAL OF THE DAY: FIND A SMALL/SHORT TERM GOAL YOU WANT TO ACHIEVE.
AFFIRMATION OF THE DAY: I CREATE MY WORLD.

X

Reflection:

CHAPTER
NINE

SELF LOVE

I THINK IT'S WEIRD HOW MOST OF US ARE SO WILLING AND ABLE TO LOVE OTHERS BETTER THAN WE LOVE OURSELVES. LIKE, WHAT IS REALLY UP WITH THAT? WHAT DO YOU SEE IN ANOTHER HUMAN THAT YOU DON'T SEE IN YOURSELF THAT YOU ARE WILLING TO GIVE THEM WHAT YOU SHOULD BE GIVING YOURSELF FIRST. I HOPE THIS DOESN'T SOUND TOO SELFISH BECAUSE THAT'S NOT WHAT THIS IS AT ALL. THIS GOES FOR ANY AND EVERYTHING. IF IT'S NOT AT ITS BEST IT'S NOT GOING TO PERFORM AT ITS BEST. YOU WOULDN'T TREAT YOUR VEHICLE LIKE CRAP AND EXPECT IT TO CONTINUE TO RUN AND GET YOU FROM A TO B WITHOUT BREAKING DOWN EVENTUALLY. SAME FOR US. WE HAVE TO START WITH SELF. I WORK ON MYSELF AND LOVE MYSELF FIRST JUST SO I CAN GIVE MY BEST. IN THE BEGINNING IT WAS A BATTLE WITH ME FEELING SELFISH IN SOME WAYS, BUT THE MORE YOU UNDERSTAND HOW IMPORTANT SELF LOVE IS, IT WILL GET EASIER. IT CAN BE SOMETHING AS SIMPLE AS A GIVING YOURSELF A FACIAL OR BUYING YOURSELF A BICYCLE LIKE YOU'VE BEEN SAYING YOU'RE GOING TO DO. IF YOU FEEL IT WOULD TRULY MAKE YOU HAPPY DO IT. AS LONG AS IT'S NOT HARMFUL TO YOU OR ANYONE ELSE.

WORD OF THE DAY: ORDER
GOAL OF THE DAY: DO SOMETHING THAT MAKES YOU HAPPY.
AFFIRMATION OF THE DAY: I LOVE ME FIRST.

Reflection:

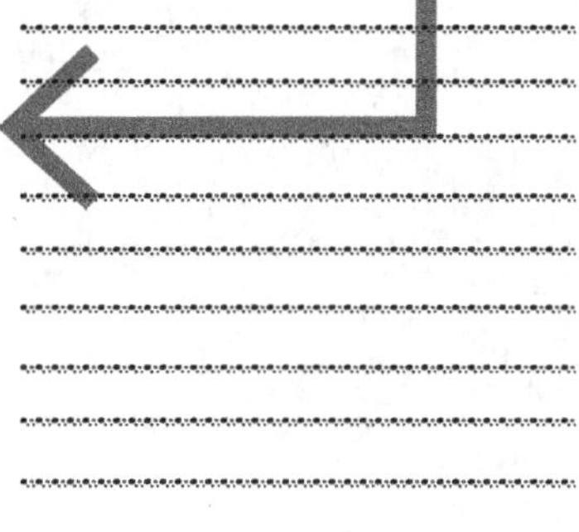

CHAPTER TEN

FOCUS

A LOT OF TIMES I BITE OFF MORE THAN I CAN CHEW. I KNOW I'M NOT ALONE. I TOO HAD TO LEARN HOW TO FOCUS ON ONE THING AT A TIME. YOU KNOW THAT SAYING ABOUT WHATEVER YOU FOCUS ON WILL GROW. SO TRUE. YOU CAN FOCUS ON MORE THAN ONE THING AT ONCE, BUT THEY WILL GROW AT A SLOWER PACE THAN IF YOU WERE TO PUT MORE ATTENTION ON ONE THING AT A TIME. OF COURSE I AM REFERRING TO GOALS AND THINGS YOU WANT TO CHANGE AND ACHIEVE IN LIFE. (PLEASE DON'T NEGLECT YOUR CHILDREN OR PETS TO ACHIEVE A GOAL QUICKER. HA HA HA I KID I KID). ALL JOKES ASIDE STAYING FOCUSED IS ANOTHER "SUPERPOWER". USE IT.

WORD OF THE DAY: ATTENTION
GOAL OF THE DAY: PICK A TASK THAT YOU HAVE BEEN PUTTING OFF AND GIVE THEM A CERTAIN AMOUNT OF ATTENTION FOR A CERTAIN AMOUNT OF TIME.
AFFIRMATION OF THE DAY: (FILL IN THE BLANK) WILL GET MY ATTENTION TODAY.

Reflection:

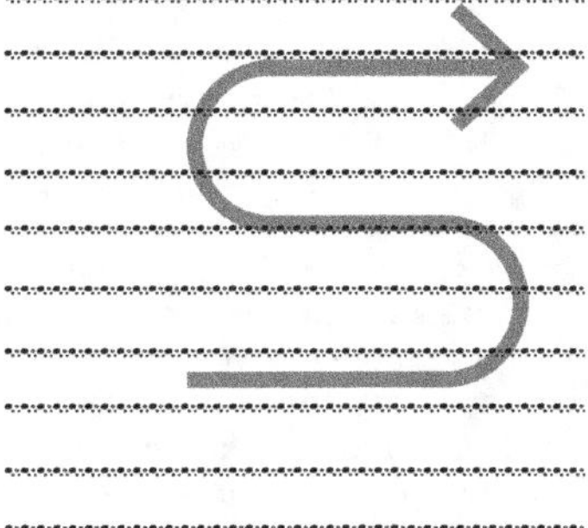

CHAPTER ELEVEN

TRUST YOURSELF

WITH ANY OTHER RELATIONSHIP TRUST IS, IF NOT THE MOST IMPORTANT; ONE OF THE MOST IMPORTANT PARTS IN BEING SUCCESSFUL. IT'S THE FOUNDATION OF WHAT YOU'RE BUILDING. SO LET'S BUILD. IT'S TIME TO BET ON YOURSELF. FIGURE OUT WHAT YOU WANT YOUR LIFE TO LOOK LIKE, UNDERSTAND IT'S NOT GONNA HAPPEN OVERNIGHT. WRITE DOWN YOUR GOALS, KNOCK OUT THE SMALLER ONES FIRST TO BUILD A LITTLE MOMENTUM AND INSPIRATION. AS I MENTIONED BEFORE CONFIDENCE IS A SUPER POWER. IT'S INVISIBLE, BUT VISIBLE. IT'S THAT THING THAT YOU NOTICE ON A PERSON WHEN THEY WALK INTO A ROOM AND EVERYONE NOTICES THEM. IT'S SPIRITUAL EVEN. I CAN HAVE $2.53 IN MY POCKET AND $5.17 IN THE BANK, BUT THE WAY I CARRY MYSELF YOU WOULD THINK I WAS A MULTI-MILLIONAIRE. THAT'S BECAUSE MONEY DOESN'T MAKE ME. I KNOW WHO I AM. I KNOW MY WEAKNESSES. I KNOW MY STRENGTHS. I KNOW WHAT I HAVE TO OFFER. THE LACK OF ONE THING CAN'T MAKE ME FEEL USELESS OR WORTHLESS. I HAVE TOO MANY OTHER THINGS GOING FOR MYSELF. RECOGNIZE YOUR STRENGTHS, STRENGTHEN YOUR WEAKNESSES. YOU WILL NEVER BE PERFECT AT EVERYTHING (SORRY), SO JUST BE GOOD A LOT OF THEM.

WORD OF THE DAY: TRUST

GOAL OF THE DAY: MAKE A CONSCIOUS DECISION TO TRUST THE PROCESS

AFFIRMATION OF THE DAY: I GOT THIS!!!

Reflection:

CONCLUSION

OKAY, SO TO WRAP THINGS UP, WE ALL HAVE INSECURITIES. I PROMISE. NO MATTER HOW BEAUTIFUL OR HOW HANDSOME YOU THINK A PERSON IS THEY ARE DEALING WITH INSECURITIES. GIVE YOURSELF A PASS TO BE IMPERFECT. IF THERE ARE THINGS YOU WANT TO CHANGE ABOUT YOURSELF MAKE THOSE CHANGES. ONE STEP AT A TIME. IF THERE ARE THINGS YOU SIMPLY CAN'T CHANGE, FIND A WAY TO ACCEPT THEM AND MAYBE EVEN GROW TO LOVE THEM. BE COMFORTABLE WITH YOUR DECISIONS. IF YOU LIKE IT WHO CARES WHO DON'T. PUT AN IMAGINARY PRICE TAG ON YOURSELF AND WALK WITH THAT PRICE TAG IN MIND EVERYWHERE YOU GO. MAKE SURE THAT SH*T IS EXPENSIVE TOO! YOU ARE WHAT YOU THINK YOU ARE. SO BE THAT!

WORD OF THE DAY: ACTION
GOAL OF THE DAY: DECIDE WHAT YOUR IMAGINARY PRICE TAG WILL BE.
AFFIRMATION: IM A BOSS AND I DO BOSS SH*T!

XIV